Where Animals Live

I0867865

# Animals in the Ocean

By John Wood

KidHaven PUBLISHING

Published in 2018 by
**KidHaven Publishing, an Imprint of Greenhaven Publishing, LLC**
353 3rd Avenue
Suite 255
New York, NY 10010



Designer: Matt Rumbelow
Editor: Holly Duhig

**Cataloging-in-Publication Data**

Names: Wood, John.
Title: Animals in the ocean / John Wood.
Description: New York : KidHaven Publishing, 2018. | Series: Where animals live | Includes index.
Identifiers: ISBN 9781534523746 (pbk.) | 9781534523722 (library bound) | ISBN 9781534525153 (6 pack) | ISBN 9781534523739 (ebook)
Subjects: LCSH: Marine animals–Juvenile literature.
Classification: LCC QL122.2 W66 2018 | DDC 591.77–dc23

Printed in the United States of America

CPSIA compliance information: Batch #CW18KL: For further information contact Greenhaven Publishing LLC, New York, New York at 1-844-317-7404.

Please visit our website, www.greenhavenpublishing.com. For a free color catalog of all our high-quality books, call toll free 1-844-317-7404 or fax 1-844-317-7405.

**Photo credits: Abbreviations: l-left, r-right, b-bottom, t-top, c-center, m-middle.**
Covertl – Boris Pamikov; Covertm – unterwegs; Covertr – Greg Amptman; Coverbl – Krzysztof Odziomek; Coverbr – Atomic Roderick.
2 – Andrey_Kuzmin. 4 – Tischenko Irina. 5: bg – Rich Carey; tl – Christopher Wood; tr – mspoli; m – Galyna Andrushko; bl – Rusla Ruseyn; br – givaga.
6 – BMJ. 8 – Seaphotoart. 9 – Brian Kinney. 10 – Tim Balcomb. 11 – Krzysztof Odziomek. 12 – Greg Amptman. 13 – Greg Amptman. 14 – Atomic Roderick.
15 – solarseven. 16 – unterwegs. 17 – Beverly Speed. 18 – Oleg Milyutin. 19 – Boris Pamikov. 20 – Andreas Altenburger. 21 – Rich Carey.
22 – bernd.neeser. 23 – Willyam Bradberry.
Images are courtesy of Shutterstock.com, with thanks to Getty Images, Thinkstock Photo, and iStockphoto.

# CONTENTS



Words that look like **this** can be found in the glossary on page 24.

# WHAT IS A HABITAT?

A habitat is a place where an animal lives. It provides the animal with food, shelter, and everything else it needs to survive.

There are many different habitats in the world. Each one is home to several different animals.

The Arctic

rain forests

mountains

forests

deserts

# WHAT ARE OCEANS?

Oceans are large areas of water between **continents**. Ocean water is called salt water, because it contains a lot of salt.

Almost three-quarters of the Earth's surface is covered by oceans.

There are five different oceans in the world. Their names are the Arctic, Atlantic, Indian, Pacific, and Southern oceans. Together they are called the World Ocean.

## TYPES OF

# OCEAN HABITAT

There are many habitats in the ocean. Big animals often live in the open ocean. Smaller animals often live in shallow waters. Some animals live in ocean trenches.

Corals are living things that are hard and stony. A group of corals together make a coral reef. Many creatures make their homes here.

The Great Barrier Reef, Australia

# CLOWNFISH

Clownfish make their homes among the tentacles of an **anemone**. An anemone lives in a coral reef and stings most animals, but not clownfish.

Clownfish clean their homes by eating the **algae** that grows on the anemones. They protect their homes by chasing away other fish that might want to eat the anemone.

# SIXGILL SHARKS

Sixgill sharks live deep down in the ocean where light doesn't reach. They have big eyes that glow bright green in the dark to help them see.

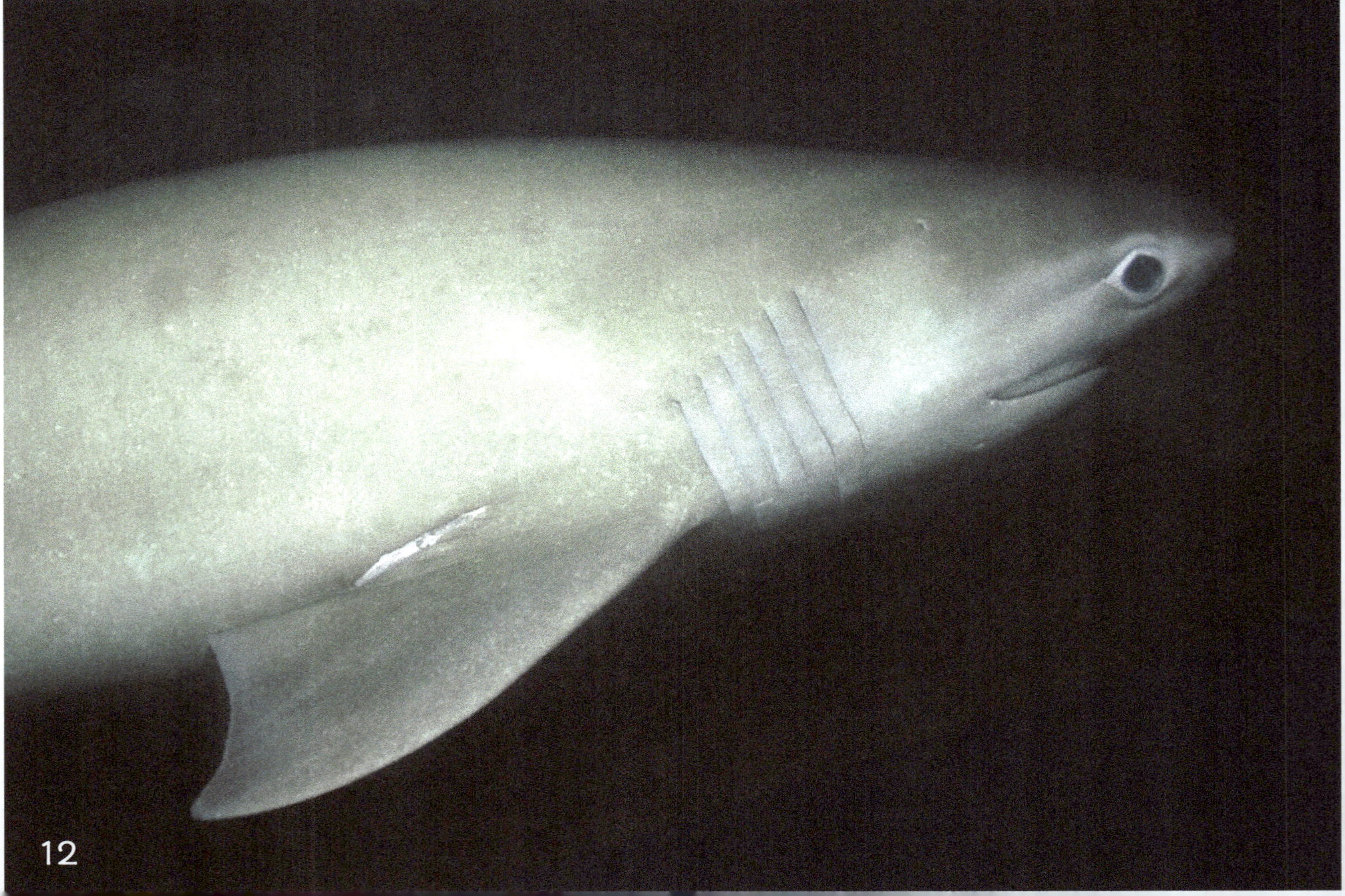

At night, these sharks will swim near the ocean's surface to hunt and **scavenge**. They usually eat animals like rays, crabs, and other sharks.

Baby sharks, like this one, are called pups.

# BLUE WHALES

Blue whales are the biggest animals on Earth. They eat tiny animals called krill. Sometimes they eat up to 40 million krill a day.

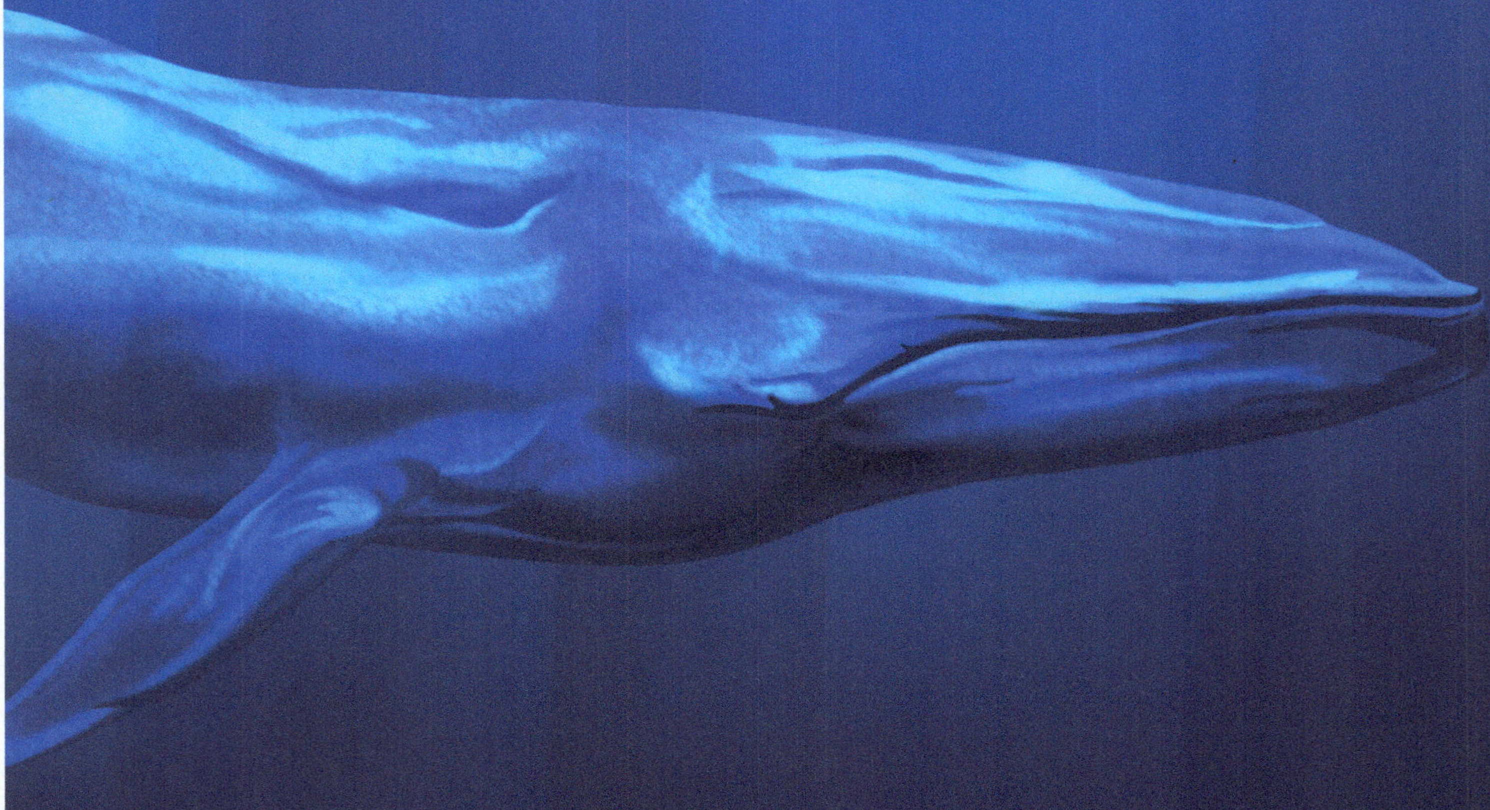

The biggest animals need the biggest homes. This is why whales live in the open ocean. They can call to other whales who are hundreds of miles away.

# MANTIS SHRIMPS

Mantis shrimps make their homes in **burrows** on the ocean floor. They often stand in front of their burrow, attacking any animal that comes near it.

When attacking, mantis shrimps use club-like claws to smash the shells of animals like crabs and sea snails.

# JELLYFISH

Jellyfish have many different homes all over the ocean. Some live deep in the dark ocean trenches and some live near the coast.

Some jellyfish glow in the dark.

Jellyfish generally move by floating along ocean currents. To catch their **prey**, jellyfish drag their tentacles around them, which sting any animals they touch.

# OCEANS IN DANGER

Our ocean animals are in danger because of overfishing. Overfishing happens when people catch and eat too many fish. This can cause some animals to become **endangered**.

Lots of waste is dumped in the ocean, like plastic bags and bottles. This waste can harm ocean animals that try to eat it.

# SCALLOPED HAMMERHEADS

Scalloped hammerheads are endangered because of overfishing. People catch these sharks for their fins to make shark fin soup.

# SEA TURTLES

Endangered sea turtles often mistake pieces of plastic for jellyfish, which they like to eat. When turtles accidentally eat plastic, they can get sick and die.

You can help keep ocean animals safe by recycling your plastic waste.

## GLOSSARY

**algae** living things that are like plants, but have no roots, stems, leaves or flowers

**anemone** an animal with tentacles that is usually fixed to something hard like a coral reef

**burrow** a hole or tunnel dug by an animal

**continent** a large area of land made up of many countries

**endangered** when a species of animal is in danger of going extinct

**ocean trench** a huge, narrow cut in the ocean floor that goes deep

**open ocean** an area of ocean far away from any land

**prey** animals that are hunted by other animals for food

**scavenge** to feed on animals that are already dead

**shelter** protection from danger and harsh weather

## Index